This Is Our Church

A Guide for Children

James A. Comiskey

Illustrated by
James Powers

A Liturgical Press Book

 THE LITURGICAL PRESS
Collegeville, Minnesota

www.litpress.org

Cover design by James Powers.

1   2   3   4   5   6   7   8

ISBN 0-8146-2597-5

Contents

Dear Reader,

One of the greatest adventures in our life is the on-going adventure of learning.

The adventure of our God relationship is a unique part of the total picture of our learning. Learning about God and the things of God is an inexhaustible pursuit, and it begins very simply.

For most of us our parents share God with us from the beginning, and we want to learn more.

I was caught up in the adventure of one part of God-learning when we began a building project at our Church. The children were as interested in the building as the adults were. The children had questions and comments.

This Is Our Church began as a response to the children. The children in this book really exist. In each family

there was a brother and a sister. They discussed and explained church to one another. As I shared their conversations and questions, I discovered that there were many boys and girls with questions.

They were not really sure why Catholics do what they do when they come together. The children wanted the right names for places. They wanted to know why we do certain actions at certain moments. The place and the people called Church were important, and they wanted to be at home in that place and with those people.

This Is Our Church is for every boy and girl who has wondered about Church and the places within the church building and the actions that we do together. We all want the right words for what we see. We want to know the right way to express what is happening.

I hope *This Is Our Church* becomes part of your adventure of learning more about God, our worship space, and the actions of worship.

Monsignor Comiskey

Our Church

Tim: It's Sunday!

Margie: And it's time to go celebrate Mass at our church.

Tim: Dad said Christians have been going to church ever since the time of Jesus.

Margie: Did they have buildings just like ours?

Tim: No, the first Christians would meet together in each others' homes.

Margie: Is that how they went to church?

Tim: Yes, going to church is about people getting together and praising God. That's really Church.

Margie: But this building is also called a church, isn't it?

Tim: Yes, it is. The building where the "gathering of people" takes place is also called a church.

Margie: I like getting together with other people for God.

The Doors

Nicole: The doors to our church are big. Can you open them?

Daniel: Sure I can open them. Not only are they big, they are very special.

Nicole: Why are they special? We have doors at our house. Are these doors different?

Daniel: Last week our Sunday School teacher told us a story in which Jesus said, "I am the door."

Nicole: Jesus is a door?

Daniel: Jesus is like a door. A door opens and lets you in. Jesus opens the way for us to go to God.

Nicole: Is that what this door does?

Daniel: This door invites us into the building which is a house for the Church.

Nicole: For the Church?

Daniel: The Church is us.

Nicole: Me, too?

Daniel: All of us. All the people. You, too.

The Atrium

Adriana: This sure is a big room.

Pio: Mom says it is called the atrium. It is our welcoming or gathering space.

Adriana: Like our family room at home?

Pio: Yes, kind of like that. We can stop and talk with our friends. We can also visit people from the parish that we might not have seen since last Sunday.

Adriana: It is also a place for us to get ready to talk to God and be with God in a special way.

Pio: That's right. But remember, here is where we are supposed to make everyone who comes to our church feel at home.

Adriana: We don't have Mass here, do we?

Pio: No, we meet and visit before and after Mass. This is an "in-between" space.

Adriana: I have heard some of the grownups call this the narthex.

Pio: This is an important place. Dad said it is almost as important as the part where we worship.

The Baptistry

Nicole: We dip our fingers in the water and make the Sign of the Cross on ourselves when we walk by the baptismal pool.

Daniel: When we were baptized, water was poured over our heads. We were baptized in the name of the Father and of the Son and of the Holy Spirit.

Nicole: Every time we walk by this water we sign ourselves again. This reminds us of our baptism.

Daniel: This space looks like a little wading pool, doesn't it?

Nicole: When adults are baptized they go down into the pool. Water is poured over their heads. It flows down over their bodies.

Daniel: Our teacher said that is the way they did baptism in the early Church.

Nicole: Can babies be lowered into the water?

Daniel: The top part of the baptismal pool is for that.

Nicole: Mom said that baptism made me a child of God in a special way. She wants me never to forget it.

Daniel: Signing ourselves with water helps us to remember that.

The Worship Space

Margie: This is the most special part of our church building, isn't it?

Tim: Yes, it's our worship space. It's the place where we celebrate Mass with our parish family.

Margie: Do you remember that Father Jim told us that the part around the altar is called the "sanctuary"?

Tim: And the rest of the space is called "the nave."

Margie: This is the space where the people are assembled.

Tim: So that's why Father sometimes calls us "the assembly."

Margie: Does Father want us to offer Mass with him?

Tim: Father wants you and me and everyone here to join in the offering that Jesus makes to our God in heaven.

Margie: Yes, every Sunday we join our priest in offering praise to God.

Tim: We listen to God's Word in the Scripture, and we praise God for the return gift of sharing in the Body and Blood of Christ Jesus.

Margie: We celebrate Mass here not only on Sunday but on other special days too, don't we?

Tim: Advent time, Christmas time, and Lenten time are special Sunday times and "other day" times.

Margie: Oh yes, and don't forget the special days of Holy Week, Easter, and the coming of the Holy Spirit at Pentecost. Some people like to come to Mass every day.

Tim: Offering praise to God with all our parish makes even the time we call "Ordinary" very special.

Margie: We celebrate other sacraments here, too. Do you remember when Aunt Kathy and Uncle Gene got married here?

Tim: Yes, they married at Mass on Saturday evening with our whole parish here.

Margie: When our neighbor Mrs. Luna died, we came here and said prayers when they brought her body to Church.

Tim: On some Sundays after Mass there are people who celebrate anointing of the sick here.

Margie: And all of these times are centered in this part of our church.

The Altar

Adriana: I told Mom that I thought our altar looked like a table. Do you know what she said?

Pio: I think I know.

Adriana: She told me that the altar in our church is the table of our Church family.

Pio: There are four of us when we eat supper at home. On special days a lot of family comes, so then the table is for all of us.

Adriana: After I make my First Communion I get to receive from the plate and the cup, too.

Pio: Our altar is very special. Dad said there should only be a cup, a plate, and a book on the altar.

Adriana: The bread is different from ordinary bread, isn't it?

Pio: It is bread that becomes the Body of Christ. The wine in the cup become the Blood of Christ.

Adriana: How's that? It still looks like bread and wine to me.

Pio: It still looks and tastes like bread and wine. The prayer of the Church and our faith tell us it is the Body and Blood of Christ.

The Presider's Chair

Tim: There's a chair near the altar.

Margie: Yes, that's the chair where Father Jim sits.

Tim: The chair is also the place from which Father presides over our worship when he is not at the altar.

Margie: He also prays certain special prayers while standing in front of the chair, doesn't he?

Tim: Mom said that those prayers are special at every Mass.

Margie: One time our class went on a visit to the courthouse. We were allowed to listen to some people having a meeting. They called the man who was leading the meeting "the chair." We thought that was funny!

Tim: That does sound strange.

Margie: Our teacher explained that the man leading the meeting was seated in front and center. His position showed that he was the one leading the meeting.

Tim: Yes, it's our priest who leads us in worship. It is not the piece of furniture in which he is seated that does the teaching and preaching and leading.

Margie: The place of the chair in front and near the altar tells us something. It says that what happens from that chair is important to our worship.

The Ambo

Nicole: That's where people stand to read from, isn't it?

Daniel: Yes, it's special because it is the place from which we hear God's living word.

Nicole: Didn't Dad say it has a special name?

Daniel: In our church we call it the ambo. It's sometimes called a pulpit.

Nicole: When I grow up I want to read from there on Sunday.

Daniel: I hope you do. But you have to do your homework. Men and women from our Church family prepare each week to be able to read God's word for all of us.

Nicole: Father Jim and Deacon Randy do, too.

Daniel: Yes, they try to give us ways to understand the words of Jesus better.

Nicole: I like it when they tell stories kids can understand.

Daniel: God's word is for all of us. I imagine the grownups can understand the kids' stories, too.

The Music Center

Adriana: I like it when we sing at church.

Pio: I like it better when the organ, piano, or the guitars play along with us.

Adriana: The night Jesus was born some angels sang.

Pio: On Sunday I wonder if we sound as good as those angels did.

Adriana: I don't know, but I'll bet Jesus likes it just as much.

Pio: Do you suppose that Jesus sang?

Adriana: Jesus sang with the apostles when they ate meals together.

Pio: That's right. At the Last Supper Jesus and the apostles sang together.

Adriana: What kind of song do you suppose they sang?

Pio: You know on Sunday the cantor sings a psalm and we all join in. Our teacher told us that Jesus and the apostles sang songs like that together.

Adriana: Do you remember one Sunday no one came to play the organ and the guitar at church?

Pio: Yes, we all sang anyway just like we do when we travel in the car with Mom and Dad.

Adriana: Before I could read I learned the "Holy, Holy" and the "Lamb of God" by heart.

Pio: Sometimes when we read the words of a new church song the words are just like a prayer.

Adriana: Of course. I'm sure that's why we sing at church. We use our voices to sing our prayers.

Pio: When the bishop came last year for Mass, our class played their recorders.

Adriana: And I got to play in the bell choir.

Pio: There are so many different and wonderful ways to praise God.

The Ambry

Tim: That case on the church wall is very beautiful.

Margie: These bottles in the case are special, aren't they?

Tim: Father told our class that the case is called an "ambry."

Margie: That's a new word.

Tim: The bottles in the case are filled with special blessed oil.

Margie: They are the containers for the holy oil used during the year in different services of the Church.

Tim: Each of the three bottles has a different set of letters on it.

Margie: Do you remember last year when we went to the cathedral? The bishop blessed the oils.

Tim: Lots of people were there from all over the diocese.

Margie: Some people from the hospital carried down the oil marked "OI." That is the oil used in the blessing of the sick.

Tim: Some of the people who were preparing to join the Church at Easter carried the oil marked "OC," the oil of catechumens.

Margie: That oil is used to bless the catechumens, those people getting ready to be baptized.

Tim: The bishop also anoints people with that oil in their confirmation. All of us were anointed with this oil in our baptism.

Margie: Maybe some day we will see the ceremony in which a new church or a new altar is dedicated, or see a priest or bishop ordained.

Tim: That's right. They use that oil marked "SC," sacred chrism. It's used for all of those special occasions.

Margie: I like the story of how David in the Old Testament was anointed to be the king.

Tim: God chose him even though he was the youngest, and the prophet anointed his head with oil.

Margie: The last time we were at Mass when a baby was baptized was the baptism of our little cousin.

Tim: Yes, Father rubbed oil on her head and he said that Jesus was anointed a priest, a prophet, and a king.

Margie: And that we are all called to share in everything that Jesus is.

The Stations of the Cross

Adriana: Do you remember during Lent when we came to Church at night for the Stations of the Cross?

Pio: We walked around the church to each station and prayed.

Adriana: The Stations of the Cross booklets had pictures from the last hours of the life of Jesus.

Pio: And we prayed the prayers and sang the songs.

Adriana: Do you remember some of the people in the story who were with Jesus?

Pio: I remember Mary, the mother of Jesus, and a woman named Veronica.

Adriana: There was Pilate, who agreed to let Jesus die, and Simon, who helped Jesus carry his cross.

Pio: There was a man named John. Jesus told John to take care of his mother, Mary.

Adriana: They did bad things to Jesus.

Pio: Then Jesus died. But he did it all because he loved us.

Adriana: Jesus didn't stay dead.

Pio: I know. God raised him from the dead. That was great.

The Reconciliation Rooms

Nicole: Are we allowed to go into these rooms?

Daniel: Yes, there's no one in them now. They are called "reconciliation rooms."

Nicole: What does that mean?

Daniel: You know. When you have an argument with someone and then you make up, you "reconcile."

Nicole: How do you do that?

Daniel: You are serious about saying "I'm sorry I did this or that" or "I didn't do this or that when I should have."

Nicole: Of course. You and Mom and Dad celebrated reconciliation last year with the kids in your class.

Daniel: When you go into the room, Father Jim is there. He represents Jesus and the whole Church. Sometimes we need to be reconciled with God and with each other.

Nicole: Father helps us? Does he give us advice?

Daniel: Yes, he acts in the name of Jesus and the Church. He helps us so we can be reconciled with God and other people if we need to be.

Nicole: And Father forgives us just as Jesus would do if he were here. Right?

Daniel: And you come away feeling wonderful!

Statues and Images

Tim: This is a beautiful statue.

Margie: Yes, it is a statue of Mary, the mother of Jesus.

Daniel: Mom told us that an angel appeared to Mary and asked her if she would become the mother of Jesus.

Nicole: The angel said, "Hail Mary full of grace, the Lord is with you." We still pray those words when we honor her.

Adriana: Statues and pictures like this help us honor and remember famous and special people.

Pio: Do you remember when we went on vacation we saw statues and pictures of famous people in different places?

Adriana: And we have pictures of relatives and friends and family at our house.

Margie: We have statues and pictures of people in our church, like this statue of Mary.

Nicole: Yes, we have them there because we honor their memory. We don't want to forget that they were people who loved God very much.

Tim, Daniel, and Pio (together):

Let's hear it for Jesus and the saints! Hurrah!

The Sacristy

Margie: Come on, Tim. We're going to help Dad get ready for Mass.

Tim: He'll be waiting for us. This is the room where they keep all the things we use during Mass.

Margie: Do I get to help get things ready again?

Tim: Of course. When Dad gets the dishes of altar breads ready, he will let us carry them to the table in the church.

Margie: There are so many cabinets and drawers. I suppose they need them so they can keep wine and candles and books here.

Tim: This is also the room where they keep the vestments, the special clothes that people wear for Mass.

Margie: Like Father Jim? And Deacon Randy?

Tim: Also the altar assistants.

Margie: And doesn't the choir keep their robes in a cabinet over there?

Tim: And you remember that on special days all the priests come here and put on their priest clothes.

Margie: This is the reason for all the cabinets and drawers. This is the "getting-ready" space.

The Blessed Sacrament Chapel

Adriana: Mom said this room is a very special place.

Pio: It's the reservation chapel of our church.

Adriana: There in the center of the chapel is a large container.

Pio: Our teacher told us that it's called a tabernacle.

Adriana: Is Christ really here?

Pio: He is here in a special way.

Adriana: How? What is kept in the tabernacle?

Pio: They keep any Communion breads that are left over after Mass.

Adriana: Why do they keep them here?

Pio: They keep them so that Father Jim and Deacon Randy can take this Communion food to sick people when they wish to receive Holy Communion.

Adriana: There are many men and women in our church who do this as well.

Pio: They take Communion to people in hospitals and nursing homes and go to wherever people live.

Adriana: I see people coming in this little chapel to pray.

Pio: People like to pray here. It's a very prayerful place.

Study Questions

Our Church_____

1. When Jesus was a baby, his parents took him to the Temple. Why did they do this? (Luke 2:22)

2. When Jesus was a boy, he went with his parents to the Temple. What happened? (Luke 2:41)

3. Where do you go to church on Sunday?

The Doors _____

1. How many doors do you have at your house?

2. What are doors for?

3. Jesus called himself a door. In some translations the word is "gate" instead of door. (John 10:9) Why would Jesus call himself a door/gate?

The Atrium

1. Another word for the gathering space at a church is "atrium." Does your church have a gathering space?

2. What is the gathering space for?

3. If you have a gathering space at your house, what do you do there?

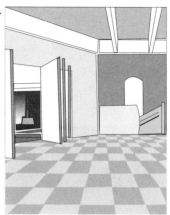

The Baptistry

1. What does it mean to "be baptized"?

2. What do we use water for?

3. Does the water in a baptism tell us something about what is happening in the mind or the heart or the soul of the person being baptized?

The Worship Space

1. What do we do in the worship space?

2. Did people who lived on our earth thousands and thousands of years ago have special places where they worshiped? How do we know?

3. For Catholics, the worship space is where they gather together to celebrate the ceremony called Mass. What is our part in the Mass?

The Altar

1. Do you have a table at your house? What do you do at that table?

2. We have a special table in the worship space. What do we call it?

3. When we are old enough, what does each of us receive from the table?

The Presider's Chair _____

1. There is a special chair in the worship space. What is it for?

2. Tell some of the different kinds of chairs that you have in your house.

3. During Mass, what does Father do at the chair?

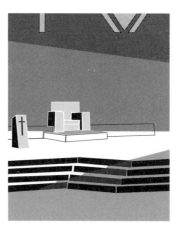

The Ambo _____

1. What is another name for the ambo?

2. Why is the ambo important?

3. Do you listen to the person who is speaking from the ambo/pulpit? Share a story that you heard from the ambo/pulpit.

The Music Center _____

1. Name the people who make music at your church.

2. What kind of instruments are used to accompany music at your church?

3. Songs at church are called hymns. Do you sing with the music? Should you sing? Why or why not?

The Ambry _____

HOLY OILS

1. Why do people use oil in their homes?

2. During what ceremonies at your church is oil used?

3. Have you ever seen an ambry in a church? Where?

Stations of the Cross _____

1. There are pictures on the walls in most Catholic churches called Stations of the Cross. What are the stations about?

2. How many stations are there? What are the names of some of the people pictured in the stations?

3. In some Catholic churches the stations are large pictures, or even large statues. Share with each other what the Stations of the Cross look like in your church or in other churches you have visited.

Reconciliation Rooms_____

1. What does the word "reconciliation" mean?

2. Who is in the reconciliation room when you go to be reconciled?

3. Share with your group any story in the Bible that tells of a time when Jesus forgave someone.

Statues and Images _____

1. Almost everyone keeps pictures of family members somewhere in their homes. Tell the names of some of the people whose pictures are in your home.

2. Have you ever seen a statue of a person who was famous in the history of our country? Where?

3. Why do we have statues and pictures of people in church?

The Sacristy _____

1. What does the word "sacristy" mean?

2. If you have been in the room in your church that is called the sacristy, what do you remember that was kept there?

3. Who are the people who help to get things ready at your church?

Blessed Sacrament Chapel _____

1. Some Catholic churches have special chapels called Blessed Sacrament chapels. What are they for?

2. There is a special place, or container, in the Blessed Sacrament chapel. What is it called?

3. What do we keep in the tabernacle?